# Getting To Know...

# Nature's Children

# COUGARS

## Katherine Grier

SCHOLASTIC INC.

New York   Toronto   London   Auckland   Sydney
Mexico City   New Delhi   Hong Kong   Buenos Aires

# Facts in Brief

**Classification of the Cougar**

> Class:    *Mammalia* (mammals)
> Order:    *Carnivora* (meat-eaters)
> Family:    *Felidae* (cat family)
> Genus:    *Felis*
> Species:    *Felis concolor*

**World distribution.**  Exclusive to North America.

**Habitat.**  Mountains, swamps, forests, river valleys.

**Distinctive physical characteristics.**  Coat in varying shades of brown with black on the back of the ears, tip of the tail, and in stripes on the muzzle; white chest and throat.

**Habits.**  Solitary; most active at night; male marks territory with scent and by scratching with its claws.

**Diet.**  Mainly deer and other fairly large mammals.

Published by Scholastic Inc.
90 Old Sherman Turnpike, Danbury, Connecticut  06816.

SCHOLASTIC and associated logos are trademarks of Scholastic Inc.

ISBN 0-7172-6697-4

Printed in the U.S.A.

*Edited by:* Elizabeth Grace Zuraw
*Photo Rights*: Ivy Images

*Photo Editor:* Nancy Norton
*Cover Design*: Niemand Design

## Have you ever wondered . . .

Sssssh! A cougar is coming! It prowls slowly and silently through the deep, dark forest. Suddenly it stops. It lets out a terrifying call that sounds like a human scream. Then, quick as a wink, it vanishes into the night.

With behavior such as this, is it any wonder that the cougar has been given the nickname of "mountain devil" and "sneak cat"? But you might be surprised to learn that it also has been called "lord of the forest" and "the greatest of wild animals." You'd almost think that people were talking about two very different animals, wouldn't you?

Just what is the truth about the cougar? Is it a sneak, or is it one of nature's truly noble creatures? The only way to solve the mystery is to look at the facts.

*Puma, panther, painter, wildcat, mountain lion—all these names are or have been used for the same animal: the cougar.*

## Soft Balls of Fur

As soon as her babies are born, a mother cougar holds each kitten with one of her huge but gentle paws and licks the baby clean and dry. Soon the kittens are snuggled up against her soft, furry belly and they're *nursing,* or drinking milk from her body. When the babies are full, they'll fall asleep by her side, curled up together for warmth.

Before long, the kittens will be spending less time sleeping. Instead, they'll be spending more time playing and tussling in between naps. All this is great fun, but it's more than that. Playing helps the kittens build up their muscles and teaches them how to pounce and grab hold of things—valuable skills they'll need when they grow up.

*Like all babies in the cat family, cougar babies are called kittens.*

## All in the Family

The cougar kittens and their mother make up one small family. But cougars are also part of a much larger family that spans the world— the cat family. Even though cougars are not small animals, *zoologists*—scientists who study animals—place them in the "small cat" branch of this well-known family. Why? Simply because cougars can't roar! They can only purr and yowl. The "big cats," such as lions, tigers, or jaguars, are just the opposite. They can't purr—but do they roar! And then there are the cheetahs. They have a branch of the cat family all to themselves. They're the only cats that can't pull in their claws!

The cougar's closest relatives in North and South America are other small cats. They're the lynx, the bobcat, and, believe it or not, the everyday ordinary house cat. You may ask, "But what about the mountain lion or puma?" Don't be fooled! Remember that these are just different names for the cougar.

*Opposite page: Adult cougars are seldom seen together, but young cougars such as these stay together for a while after leaving their mother.*

## Cougar Country

Cougars used to live in many parts of North America. How did these same animals manage to live in places as different as forests, prairies, lowlands, and mountains, and hot areas as well as cold? They managed because their needs are simple. All they need is food, such as deer and some smaller animals; a bit of cover from which to hunt; and some slight shelter from cold weather.

Cougars could once find those things in all sorts of places. But as towns and farms spread over much of the land, cougar country shrank. Now most cougars in North America live in the mountains of the West. The only place this animal now lives on the East Coast is Florida, where it is called a panther.

*Where cougars live in North America*

## One Cougar Only!

Today, most cougars live in mountainous places. The cougar's *territory,* or the area that an animal lives in and defends from other animals, is usually quite large compared to most animal territories. The territory has to be large so that the cougar can find enough food.

Once a cougar has found a territory, it guards it carefully by leaving "signs" that tell other cougars, "I live here." These signs are called *scrapes.* The cougar makes them by scraping leaves and dirt into heaps and mixing them with its urine or droppings. The cougar also scratches trees in different parts of its territory and sprays them with urine. When other cougars see and smell one of these scratching posts or a scrape, they usually go the other way rather than risk a fight.

*The cougar uses its claws to make "No Trespassing" signs in its territory.*

## Big and Powerful

The cougar is one of the biggest cats in all of North and South America. Only the jaguar is bigger. Not including the tail, an average-sized female is about 5 feet (1.5 meters) long and weighs about 90 pounds (about 40 kilograms). The male is almost twice as big.

The cougar's long, muscled legs give it lots of leaping power. Because its back legs are slightly longer than its front legs, it always looks as if it's heading downhill, even when it's standing on flat ground. If you've ever watched a house cat jump, you know that most of a cat's jumping power comes from its hind legs. It gathers its hind legs up under itself and then springs forward. Thanks to the cougar's long, strong hind legs, it can leap as far as 23 feet (7 meters) at a time. That's like jumping across a city street in a single bound!

To keep its balance as it leaps, the cougar uses its thick, heavy tail as a rudder.

*A cougar's tail may be as long as 3 feet (almost 1 meter).*

## Sneaking up on Dinner

You might expect that an animal as strong as a cougar is a strong runner, but that's not so. The cougar can run fast, but only for a short distance. Because it tires quickly, it must rely on stealth and cleverness to sneak up on *prey,* animals hunted by other animals for food.

How can an animal as big as a cougar avoid being seen as it stalks prey? The cougar's tan or tawny coloring is good *camouflage*—any feature an animal has that blends in with its surroundings and makes it difficult to see.

At first glance, a cougar may appear to be all tan, but a closer look reveals patches of white and black fur below its nose. The patches form a butterfly shape on its upper lip. The back of a cougar's ears and the tip of its tail are black, too.

If a cougar wants to let other animals know how it feels, it moves its ears and tail. The black markings draw attention to its switching tail or laid-back ears. But if a cougar doesn't want to be seen, it just keeps very still. Then the darker patches blend in with the natural shadows of its surroundings.

Opposite page: *Some people call the cougar a* catamount, *which is short for "cat of the mountain."*

## Silent Paws, Sure Claws

The cougar wouldn't be able to move so quietly and stealthily through its territory if it weren't for its broad, heavy paws. There are four toes and a thumb on each front paw and four toes on each hind paw. A leathery pad on the bottom of each toe and at the base of each paw muffles the sound of the cougar's footsteps. And the cougar can get extra traction by spreading its toes wide to grasp rough ground.

On each toe, the cougar has a little pocket that holds a very sharp, curved claw. Each claw is about as long as your big toe. When the cougar wants to move silently, it pulls its claws into these pockets. But when it wants to climb a tree or hold its prey, out pop the claws, giving the cougar a good grip.

*A cougar's front and hind paw-prints look much the same because the thumb on the front paw is higher up and so does not touch or mark the ground when the animal walks.*

*Front*

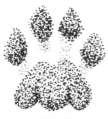

*Hind*

*A lofty perch in a tree is an ideal spot to wait for passing prey.*

## Super Sight

Like all animal hunters, the cougar must see its prey before the prey sees it. The cougar has to be able to judge distances correctly because it must know exactly how far to leap in order to catch its prey. Very keen eyesight helps the cougar spot animals that are far off. It also helps that the cougar's eyes are at the front of its head, rather than toward the sides. This helps the cougar more accurately judge how far away things are.

Deer, the cougar's main prey, have good eyesight, too. But they can't judge distances easily because their eyes are set more to the sides of their head. To a deer and other prey animals, side positioning of the eyes is helpful. It gives the animal a wider angle over which to watch for enemies. But with its prey able to keep such a good lookout, no wonder the cougar has to be a stealthy hunter!

Like many animals, cougars are *color-blind.* They see only in shades of black, white, and gray. But at night they see much better than we do, making them excellent night hunters.

*Opposite page:*
*If a cougar doesn't catch its dinner at night, it'll hunt right on through the next day. But night hunting is especially important in summer, when days are hot and most prey animals feed at night.*

# Deer for Dinner

Although the cougar's main food is deer, it hunts other animals, too. Moose, mountain goats, coyotes, bear cubs, porcupines, rabbits, birds, and mice are some of the cougar's other menu choices. One zoologist even tells of watching a cougar eat a whole meal of just grasshoppers!

Ideally, a cougar needs to eat about 9 pounds (4 kilograms) of meat a day—about as much meat as there is in 36 hamburgers! That works out to one deer every seven to ten days.

It's easy to feel sorry for the cougar's prey, but, in fact, the hunting cougar is doing an important job. In winter especially, a herd of deer may have trouble finding enough leaves, twigs, and grass to eat. The cougar kills deer that are old, weak, or sick, leaving more food for the strong, healthy deer. If the cougar didn't kill the weaker deer, the whole herd would suffer and many might die of starvation.

*When hunting, the cougar relies more on its eyes than its nose.*

## Time To Eat

Once a cougar has caught its prey, it usually likes to eat in a protected place. Often it drags its catch to a favorite eating spot or even carries it up to the branch of a tree.

When it comes to eating, the cougar is well equipped. It has special scissor-like teeth that cut the food into pieces small enough to swallow. This is important because the cougar doesn't chew its food first. Instead, it swallows whole chunks of meat. And to ensure that not a morsel of its food is wasted, the cougar's tongue has a sharp, horny surface that can scrape bones clean.

A cougar can't eat a whole deer in one meal. It takes what's left and hides it under leaves, branches, or stones. If fresh food is hard to find, the cougar will go back to this stored food many times. But if hunting is easy, it'll leave its catch after only one meal. Cougar leftovers aren't wasted. Other animals and birds eat anything the cougar leaves behind.

## Cold-weather Cougars

The cougar doesn't prepare for winter the way some animals do. It doesn't gather up supplies of food as the chipmunk does. Nor does it eat a lot of food to put on fat, and then sleep away the winter months like the woodchuck. After all, the cougar's main prey, the deer, stays out all winter, so the cougar can, too. To keep warm as it hunts, the cougar has a coat that grows longer and thicker for the winter months.

Actually, the cougar's fur coat is two coats in one. Close to its body is a thick layer of inner fur. This holds in body heat and helps keep out the cold. A second layer of long *guard hairs* on the outside sheds snow and rain.

The cougar doesn't shed its coat at a particular time of year, as some animals do. The hairs of its fur coat are shed and grow in all year long. In winter, the cougar's coat is at its longest and thickest.

*To find food, a cougar may travel up to 25 miles (40 kilometers) in a single day.*

## Hard Times, Good Times

If a winter is hard on the deer, it will be hard on the cougar, too. If there aren't enough deer, the cat must hunt smaller animals to survive. Smaller prey is just as hard to catch as deer, and the cougar must catch more of it to feed itself. And as the snow gets deeper, hunting gets harder because the cougar is heavy and sinks into the snow. Fortunately, cougars don't have to eat every day. In fact, they can go for days without a meal.

Although there are hard times for the cougar, there are good times as well, when prey is easy to find. After hunting, there is little for the cougar to do but to rest and to *groom,* or clean, itself. The big cat licks itself all over and sharpens its claws. Then it stretches out on a favorite rock or drapes itself over the branches of a favorite tree. There the cougar will spend the day dozing or basking in the sun or simply watching the world go by. However, if the cougar is a female, she may also have the busy task of raising a family.

Opposite page:
*If there's a good supply of food, winter is no problem for the cougar.*

29

## Courtship Calls

Cougars *mate,* or come together to produce young, any time of the year, but more often than not, they mate early in the winter. The female cougar leaves her home territory to look for a mate. She calls as she pads through new territories. Sometimes she meows like a house cat, only louder. And sometimes her voice rises in a scream that can be heard a long distance away.

Finally a male cougar hears her or smells her scent. He sets out to find her. If another male is following her as well, the males may fight to decide which of them will mate with the female. Usually the strongest male wins.

Male and female cougars stay together for only about two weeks. Shortly after they've mated, the female travels back to her own territory to await the arrival of her new family.

Before her young are born, the female searches for a *den,* or animal home. She might choose a tangle of tree roots or a rocky cave as a nursery for her babies.

Opposite page:
*A mother cougar raises her babies by herself. She is careful to search out a den that will be safe from enemies and bad weather.*

Overleaf:
*The two-week mating period is the only time you might see two adult cougars together.*

*This cougar kitten will lose its spots when it reaches the age of about six months.*

# Smitten with Kittens

Three months after the adults have mated, the kittens are born. There are usually two to four kittens in a *litter,* the group of babies that are born together. The babies are helpless. Their eyes are tightly shut, and they can hardly crawl. But their mother is there, and she tends to them carefully. She licks each one clean with her scratchy tongue and then settles down so that they can nestle in close to her body. Soon the babies are nursing vigorously, drinking her warm, nourishing milk.

The new kittens don't look much like their parents. You might even wonder if they belong to the same family. For one thing, they're tiny. From nose to tail, one would fit between your elbow and your fingertips. And each weighs only about as much as two big bananas!

But size isn't the only difference. The kittens' eyes, when they open, are blue, not greenish-yellow like their parents'. And their tails are stubby. Their coats are different, too—yellow-brown in color and covered with dark spots. Their parents' coats are a solid tan color.

## Tender Mother

Opposite page:
*When a mother cougar needs to move a baby, she does so by gently taking hold of the back of its neck with her mouth.*

The kittens grow quickly on their mother's rich milk. In two weeks, their eyes are open, and soon they're tumbling about. After a while, their mother brings them meat from her own catches. Soon they're eating only meat.

Except when she's hunting, the mother cougar stays with her kittens, purring happily as she watches them play and eat. But if they get too rough-and-tumble, she separates them by grabbing them by the scruff of the neck.

*Predators,* or animals that hunt other animals for food, are a threat to kittens. And bears and even male cougars hunt little kittens—if they get a chance, that is. Before letting the babies leave the den, their mother checks outside for enemies. She sniffs the air and looks around, then gives a low call if it's safe to come out. And she has a special "head for safety!" call to warn them of danger once they're outside.

From time to time, the mother has to leave her kittens to go hunting, but even then she stays nearby. Any animal that comes too close will have to face a mighty fierce and angry mother.

## The Basics

Just like all young children, cougar kittens must learn how to take care of themselves and how to fend for themselves. Cleanliness is a must, and sharp claws are essential for survival.

Cougars wash themselves the same way that house cats do. With their long, rough tongues, they lick all the dust and scraps of food from their fur. And they use a front paw, carefully licked between each wash, to clean their faces and behind their ears.

What does a cougar do when its claws get dull? Sharpen them, of course, just as you clip your nails when they get too long. A cougar's claws grow in layers from the inside out, rather like an onion. When the outside layer grows dull, the cat pulls it off by scratching on a tree. That's what your pet cat is doing when it scratches on some bark—or the furniture!

*Cougars are very careful to keep their long curved claws well sharpened.*

*This kitten has just learned that it doesn't take much skill to stalk a desert tortoise. Other prey, unfortunately, will be quite a bit harder to catch!*

## Learning the Ropes

To cougar kittens, part of learning how to survive is learning how to move quietly. When they first move around, they're always stumbling over their own big feet. But with time and practice, they become as strong and agile as acrobats and as quiet as shadows.

Cougars can move through the woods for hours without making a sound. They can climb trees and move among the branches with ease. They can spring from the ground to a tree branch or leap over a small stream. They can even swim—and swim well—if they have to.

*A cougar kitten has a lot to learn before it's ready to live on its own.*

## Practice Makes Purr-fect

Cougar kittens aren't born knowing how to hunt. They have to learn—and they start by playing. They chase their mother's tail, pounce on stray leaves, and spring out at one another.

Slowly their mother trains them in the many skills they'll need. When she brings meat to them, she teaches them to attack it before eating. When the babies are big enough to leave the den, she shows them how to stalk a rabbit and how to catch a porcupine without—ouch!—getting a pawful of quills.

When the kittens are half-grown, she takes them with her one at a time to hunt deer. That way, the kittens learn to catch animals bigger than they are and to pick out weak animals that won't kick at them with sharp hoofs. They learn to keep trying until they make a catch.

Then the kittens must practice their newly learned skills. One thing they learn very fast is that it takes a *lot* of practice to become a good hunter!

# Life Goes On

When the young cougars are about two years old, their mother starts getting grouchy. She no longer shares her food catches, and when the kittens try to play, she loses her temper and cuffs them with one of her paws. It's time for the mother cougar to start a new family, and she's letting her youngsters know it's time for them to leave and begin life on their own.

The young cougars are ready. By now, they're almost as big as their mother. They're strong and agile, and have learned to move silently as they stalk prey. And although they won't be expert hunters for some time yet, they can hunt well enough to feed themselves.

Each young cougar sets out to find a territory for itself. It can't take just any land it likes. It must find a home range where no other cougar is living or where there's a cougar so old or weak that it can easily be driven off and away.

Each young cougar will live alone and hunt alone in its new territory. In time, it will mate, and new kittens will be born, taking their place in the fascinating world of the cougar.

Opposite page:
*Young cougars can expect a life span of up to about 18 years.*

# Words To Know

**Camouflage**   Animal features that blend in with the animal's surroundings.

**Den**   An animal home.

**Groom**   To clean or brush fur or feathers.

**Guard hairs**   Long coarse hairs that make up the outer layer of the cougar's and some other animals' coats.

**Litter**   Young animals born together.

**Mate**   To come together to produce young. Either member of an animal pair is also called the other's mate.

**Nurse**   To drink milk from the mother's body.

**Predator**   An animal that hunts other animals for food.

**Prey**   An animal hunted by other animals for food.

**Scrapes**   Piles of leaves, urine, and droppings used to mark the boundaries of a territory.

**Territory**   The area that an animal or group of animals lives in and often defends from other animals of the same kind.

**Zoologist**   A scientist who studies animals.

# Index

PHOTO CREDITS
**Cover:** Stephen J. Krasemann, *Valan Photos.* **Interiors:** Tim Fitzharris, 4. /*Valan Photos:* Stephen J. Krasemann, 7, 11, 20, 22, 25, 26, 30, 38, 41, 43, 44; Hälle Flygare, 19; Gerhard Kahrmann, 32-33; Thomas Kitchin, 46. /*Thomas Stack & Associates:* Thomas Kitchin, 8. /*Ivy Images/Spectrum Stock:* J. Dawson, 12. /*Ivy Images:* Lynn Rogers, 15, 16; Don Johnston, 28; Alan & Sandy Carey, 34. /*Visuals Unlimited:* P. Lindholm, 37.

# Getting To Know...

# Nature's Children

# EAGLES

## Merebeth Switzer

SCHOLASTIC INC.

New York   Toronto   London   Auckland   Sydney
Mexico City   New Delhi   Hong Kong   Buenos Aires

# Facts in Brief

**Classification of North American eagles**

Class: *Aves* (birds)

Order: *Falconiformes* (falcon-like birds)

Family: *Accipitridae*

Genus: *Haliaeetus* (includes the Bald Eagle)
*Aquila* (includes the Golden Eagle)

Species: *Haliaeetus leucocephalus* (Bald Eagle)
*Aquila chrysaetos* (Golden Eagle)

**World distribution.** The Bald Eagle is exclusive to North America; Golden Eagles are found in Europe, Asia, northern Africa, and North and Central America.

**Habitat.** Varies with species.

**Distinctive physical characteristics.** Sharp hooked beak; curved talons; large wingspan.

**Habits.** Usually mates for life; will maintain and re-use nests year after year; is active only during the day.

**Diet.** Bald Eagles live on fish; Golden Eagles eat other birds and small mammals.

Published by Scholastic Inc.
90 Old Sherman Turnpike, Danbury, Connecticut 06816.

SCHOLASTIC and associated logos are trademarks of Scholastic Inc.

ISBN 0-7172-6697-4

Printed in the U.S.A.

*Edited by:* Elizabeth Grace Zuraw
*Photo Rights*: Ivy Images

*Photo Editor:* Nancy Norton
*Cover Design*: Niemand Design

# Have you ever wondered . . .

# Eagles

No wonder many people consider the eagle the king of birds. It's one of the biggest and most powerful birds in the world.

Opposite page: *The Bald Eagle is probably North America's most admired bird.*

Through the ages, people everywhere have linked eagles with power and dignity. The Greek gods were said to take the form of eagles when they visited Earth. Roman, Russian, Austrian, and French emperors used the eagle as an emblem of their empires' might. Native people in North America have treasured eagle feathers as symbols of power and strength. And the Bald Eagle is the national bird of the United States.

But like many powerful animals, eagles have been feared as well as admired. How do you view eagles? Do you think of them as fierce hunters? Or do you see them as beautiful, majestic birds with their own role to play in the natural world? Read on to find out if either—or both—of these views is true of the fabled and mysterious eagle.

## First Flight

Opposite page: *These two young eagles may soon be ready to take the plunge into their first flight.*

The gawky young eagle peers from the edge of its nest. Its mother waits nearby, her feathers gleaming in the mid-morning sun. For many weeks, the chick has demanded constant attention from its parents, but the time has come for it to learn the skills it will need to live on its own.

Learning to fly is a little like learning to walk. It doesn't happen with the first try. It takes lots of practice, and many bumps and false landings. While the young eagle perches nervously on the nest, its mother calls to it encouragingly in high-pitched squeaks. In her claws she clutches some meat. Food is very important to young eagles, and this one is hungry. But the mother won't budge. To eat, the young eagle must fly to her.

The chick hops timidly, wings outstretched, to the very edge of the nest. Then, with a less than graceful tumble, it *fledges,* or takes its first flight.

## Eagles Everywhere

Eagles are found on every continent except Antarctica. Some live in desert areas, and others live in swamps and jungles. Still others live in forests or high in the mountains or along the shores of large lakes and oceans.

Although there are 59 different kinds of eagles in the world, only two kinds live in North America. These are the Golden Eagle and the Bald Eagle.

*The Golden Eagle is a native of Europe, Asia, and North America. In North America, it lives mainly in the mountainous regions of the West.*

## Eagle Relatives

Just like their very close relatives, the hawks, eagles are known as *birds of prey,* birds that eat meat and hunt other animals for food. Other birds of prey are vultures, owls, and giant condors.

What do birds of prey have in common? Like all flying birds, their bodies are covered with feathers, their bones are hollow, and their young hatch from eggs. But they also have several special features that help them hunt.

They have large, hooked beaks that are especially strong and suited for tearing meat. Their feet, built for grabbing, come equipped with sharp claws called *talons.* And they all have very powerful wings and flight muscles that enable them to catch food and carry it away while they're on the move.

*The eagle's large curved beak identifies it as a bird of prey.*

*With more than 7,000 feathers, the Bald Eagle has to do a careful job of* preening, *using its beak to clean, smooth, and rearrange its feathers.*

## Hawk or Eagle?

At a distance, you might get eagles and some kinds of hawks mixed up because their shapes are similar. But if you could see a hawk and an eagle side by side, you could tell who's who right away. How?

*Red-tailed Hawk*

North American eagles are at least twice as big as the largest hawks. An eagle has a body length of about 30 to 40 inches (about 75 to 100 centimeters) and a wingspan of up to about 7.5 feet (about 230 centimeters).

*Bald Eagle*

Another difference is the size of the eagle's beak. If you look at the profile of an eagle, you'll notice that its beak is nearly as long as its head. A hawk's beak might be big, but it's not as big as an eagle's!

*This young Bald Eagle's beak will remain black until the bird is about three years old. At that time, the beak will turn a beautiful golden color.*

## Light But Strong

Why can't you fly? One of the many reasons is your weight. Like most animals, you have solid bones and muscles and are simply too heavy to get off the ground, no matter how hard you flap your arms. But birds are amazingly light for their size, mainly because their bones are hollow. If you were to weigh an eagle and a dog that are the same size, you'd find that the eagle weighs much, much less than the dog.

Because the eagle often carries its dinner in its talons as it flies, this bird has to be strong as well as light. Its bones must be extra sturdy. Many eagle bones have a mesh of cross-ribs inside the bone to reinforce it in much the same way that steel rods reinforce skyscrapers and bridges.

*The skeleton of the mighty eagle is very light, weighing just over half a pound (270 grams).*

## Feathers for all Functions

Next time you see a feather on the ground, take a close look at it and see if you can figure out what part of the bird's body it came from. Is it a tail feather? A wing feather? Each type of feather on a bird's body has a special job to do. Let's take a closer look at an eagle and see how its feathers work.

The eagle's wing feathers help it fly. Some of these flight feathers overlap to form a broad paddle that pushes air down and back as the eagle flaps. Other wing feathers can be spread or lifted to help the bird speed up or slow down.

The eagle's body feathers are smaller. They fit together tightly to streamline the eagle so that it can glide more easily through the air.

Underneath the body feathers are very soft, fluffy feathers called *down.* These feathers hold in body heat to keep the eagle warm in cold weather. To cool off in hot weather, the eagle holds its feathers upright, allowing body heat to escape.

Opposite page:
*On a 9-pound (about 4 kilograms) eagle, the feathers weigh about 1.5 pounds (.68 kilograms). The same eagle's skeleton weighs less than half of that!*

## Feather Boots

Most eagles have feathers covering all of their bodies except for the beak and legs. But one group of eagles have feathers on their legs, too. Because their feathered legs make them look as if they're wearing boots, they're called—what else?—*booted eagles.* The Golden Eagle is a member of this group.

*Feather-legged booted eagles are the most numerous and common of the eagles in North America.*

## Feet To Fit the Food

You may not think of toes as being terribly important, but toes are crucial to the eagle. Without its grasping toes and sharp talons, the eagle couldn't grab onto its dinner.

An eagle's foot has four toes—three towards the front and one at the back. The single back toe can come forward to touch the front toes, much the way your thumb can touch your other fingers. This helps the eagle grasp things.

All eagles have four toes and sharp talons, but each kind of eagle has slightly different feet, depending on what it hunts. The Bald Eagle, for instance, eats mostly fish. If you've ever tried to hold onto a slippery, squirming fish, you know how difficult it is. To give it a better grip, the Bald Eagle's toes are covered with rough bumps that make it harder for a fish to slip through them. The Golden Eagle, on the other hand, hunts mostly small animals. Its toes are small but very strong. Once in its grasp, a Golden Eagle's prey is not likely to escape.

*Opposite page: Fish is the favorite food of the Bald Eagle.*

*An eagle's talons grip so well that the bird is in no danger of falling off its perch even when it sleeps.*

## Ruler of the Skies

The eagle can glide for long periods of time without having to flap its long, broad wings. How? Like many other large birds, it's an expert at hitching a ride on *thermals,* or rising currents of warm air. It glides up on the warm air currents that rise from the ground or it makes use of the upward movement of air passing up and over mountains and other landforms.

Using rising air currents, an eagle can soar more than 2 miles (about 3 kilometers) above the ground. That's a long way up!

Eagles aren't the fastest birds around, but in a dive they can reach speeds of about 100 miles (about 160 kilometers) per hour. They dive to snatch food off the ground or from the water, but sometimes they seem to dive and swoop through the air just for the fun of it.

*Wing slots at the tips of an eagle's wings help the bird steer while it soars.*

# Old Eagle Eyes

Eagles hunt by day, using their sharp eyes to zero in on their prey. The eagle's eyes face forward the same as yours do. Just as you can tell exactly where to reach to pick up a sandwich, the eagle can judge exactly where to pounce to catch its meal. That's important because, unlike your sandwich, the eagle's dinner often is on the move.

An eagle's eyesight is superb. It can clearly see things that would look like a faint blur in the distance to you or that would be too far for you to see at all. Some *naturalists*—people who study animals and plants—believe that an eagle can even detect something as small as a rabbit from as far away as 2 miles (nearly 3 kilometers)!

Because the eagle has such sharp eyesight, it can fly over fields, forests, and lakes, and watch for any small movements far below. At that great distance, the eagle can't be seen by the prey, so it doesn't scare it away, making the meal all the easier to catch.

*Opposite page: An eagle's intense gaze and keen eyesight explain why it's a real compliment to be told you have an "eagle eye."*

## Safety Goggles

Have you ever crossed a beach in a high wind, and had to choose between getting your eyes full of sand or finding your way? Envy the eagle. It can close its eyes and still see where it's going!

An eagle's eyes are a very important part of its hunting equipment. Without them, the bird would starve. To keep its eyes from being injured, the eagle has three protective lids for each eye. Like you, it has ordinary top and bottom eyelids, but it also has a special see-through eyelid that slides sideways across each eye. This eyelid, called a *nictitating membrane,* cleans and moistens the eye as it moves across it, and can be closed to protect the eye from dust and danger.

*Though an eagle is much smaller than you are, its eyes are larger than yours!*

# Pellet Puzzles

Like most birds of prey, eagles aren't dainty eaters. Rather than carefully pick the flesh from a bone the way you do with a piece of chicken, the eagle swallows every bit of its food—fur, feathers, scales, bones, and all.

While eating this way would cause problems for most of us, it's no problem for an eagle. This bird's stomach works to sort out the good food from the pieces that are of no value. The parts that can't be digested are coughed up by the eagle in the form of hard, neat little pellets that are about the size of small sausages. By studying these pellets, naturalists can find out what foods the eagle has been eating.

*Eagles have to travel many miles each day in search of food. In the fall, Bald Eagles may travel thousands of miles in search of a warm place with open water where fish can be easily hunted.*

## Fish Feast

Eagles usually live alone, flying and hunting by themselves or with their mates. There are times, however, when dozens of eagles get together. No, they're not being sociable. They're fishing! You might see groups of Bald Eagles near rivers where salmon are spawning. The salmon are weak and tired from their long journey to their spawning grounds. That makes them easy catches for the hungry birds.

Usually, though, each eagle has its own home *territory,* or area that the bird lives, hunts, and nests in, and defends from other eagles. The size of an eagle's territory depends on the amount of food available and the supply of good nesting sites.

*The largest number of wintering Bald Eagles is found in Alaska. In the fall, as many as 3,000 of them gather there. They live in large groups and feed on salmon.*

## Monster Nests

Eagles usually mate for life, and they begin their families in the early spring. Normally, a pair of eagles uses the same nest year after year. So when they build it, they build it to last.

The nests are made of large sticks and small branches that are patiently gathered one by one. After the base is finished, smaller twigs, bark, weeds, and leaves are added. Year after year, the nest grows bigger. After it's been in use for a few years, it's enormous. One Bald Eagle nest was found to be nearly 20 feet (6 meters) deep and about 10 feet (almost 3 meters) across the top. Even more amazing, it weighed nearly 6,000 pounds (about 2,700 kilograms). That's heavier than many cars!

Eagles build their nests in safe places, away from hungry egg snatchers. Bald Eagles often choose nest sites in the tops of tall trees, and often the site is near water. Golden Eagles often build their nests on ledges in the mountains. They sometimes build several nests in their territory, but use only one at a time.

*Opposite page: An eagle nest could well outlast its original owners. It may then be taken over by another pair of eagles.*

## A Small Family

Because baby eagles require a lot of care, the mother lays only one to three eggs. She'd be unable to care for a larger family. For 28 to 35 days, the mother *broods* the eggs, or sits on them to keep them warm until they hatch. Her mate stays nearby during this time, and brings her food. He may even share in the brooding. Later, when the babies hatch, it'll take a lot of work from both parents to care for their family.

*Finding food for a growing family keeps an eagle parent pretty busy.*

# The Hard Work of Hatching

If you could eavesdrop on an eagle nest, you might be in for a surprise. Often, when the babies are ready to hatch, they can be heard chirping inside their eggs!

Like most creatures that hatch from eggs, the eagle chick, or *eaglet,* has a special *egg tooth,* or point on the tip of its beak. The chick uses this hard tooth-like point to break through the tough shell of its egg. After the baby hatches, the egg tooth becomes loose and falls off.

Hatching is hard work. It may take up to two days for an eaglet to hammer its way out of its egg. When it finally flops out of the shell, it lies still, exhausted by the effort of hatching. Its downy feathers are still moist from the liquid inside the egg, but the eaglet dries quickly. Soon the small ball of down is flopping around in the nest.

Opposite page: *Whether their nest is inland or on a seacoast, all baby eagles spend their time the same way: chirping, sleeping, and waiting for the next meal.*

## Feeding Time

Now the hard work begins for the eaglets' parents. They soon discover that their little white fluff-balls are all stomach. The babies' loud chirping calls tell the parents that they want food and they want it now! It always seems to be time for a meal, and for the next ten weeks or so, both parents will be kept very busy catching food for themselves and their growing family.

Eagles are gentle parents. They patiently tear off tiny pieces of meat and feed the little chunks one by one to their chicks. Gradually the pieces get bigger as the eaglets grow bigger.

*Eaglets weigh only about 3 ounces (85 grams) when they hatch. By about 12 weeks of age, these eaglets will have all their feathers, though they won't yet be able to fly.*

## Growing, Growing, Grown

Constant eating helps the eaglets grow quickly. Within 45 days, they weigh nearly 40 times what they did at hatching. If a human baby grew at this rate, a seven-week-old would weigh nearly 300 pounds (more than 130 kilograms)! But baby eagles don't continue to grow at this rate. If they did, they'd soon weigh too much to fly.

*This young eagle has a way to go before it gets its grown-up feathers. But even at this early age, it has the majestic appearance for which its family of birds is known.*

## Leaving Mom and Dad

By three months of age, the eaglets have shed their fluffy down and have grown a new set of feathers more suited for the business of flying. But before their first flight, they practice hopping up and down in their nest and flapping their wings. And they watch their parents take off and land to see how it's done. Then, one day, urged on by their tired parents, they're out of the nest and flying.

By the end of the summer, the young eaglets have become skilled hunters. They now are ready to go off on their own. Some are nervous about leaving, but their parents drive them off. There simply isn't enough food in one territory for parents and young eagles, too.

*After leaving the nest, young eagles remain with their parents for a few weeks while they perfect their hunting and flying skills.*

# New Clothes

During their first three or four years of life, young Golden and Bald Eagles are both brown and look very much alike. However, the Golden Eagle has lighter markings on the underside of its wings and tail.

Like all birds, the young eagles *molt*—they lose their feathers and grow new ones every year. As they mature, the Bald Eagles begin to grow their distinctive *plumage,* the covering of feathers on a bird. By about four years of age, male and female Bald Eagles have beautiful white feathers on their heads and tails. In this case, *bald* doesn't mean "featherless." Rather, it means "white."

Golden Eagles also change color as they grow up, but not as much as Bald Eagles. The golden-brown color remains, but the light parts under the wings and tail darken.

The young eagles have now reached the point in their lives where they're ready to start their own families. With luck, they may live to be 20 years old in the wild and raise many hungry, chirping eaglets of their own.

*Opposite page: Don't be fooled! This isn't a Golden Eagle. It's a young Bald Eagle—before its white head feathers have grown in. You can see touches of white on its neck.*

# Words To Know

**Bird of prey**   A bird that hunts other animals for food.

**Booted eagles**   Eagles with feathered legs that make the bird look as if it's wearing boots.

**Brood**   To sit on eggs to keep them warm as the young develop inside.

**Down**   Very soft, fluffy feathers.

**Eaglet**   A baby eagle.

**Egg tooth**   A hard point on an eaglet's beak that it uses to break out of its shell.

**Fledge**   To take a first flight.

**Hatch**   To break out of an egg.

**Mate**   To come together to produce young.

**Molt**   To lose one set of feathers and grow another to replace them.

**Naturalists**   People who study animals and plants.

**Nictitating membrane**   A see-through eyelid that protects and cleans an eagle's eye.

**Plumage**   The covering of feathers on a bird.

**Preening**   Using the beak to clean, smooth, and rearrange the feathers.

**Prey**   An animal hunted by another animal for food.

**Talon**   The claw of an eagle, owl, or other bird of prey.

**Thermal**   A rising current of warm air.

**Territory**   An area that an animal or group of animals lives in and often defends from other animals of the same kind.

# Index

PHOTO CREDITS
**Cover:** Stephen J. Krasemann, *Valan Photos*. **Interiors:** *Ivy Images:* Alan & Sandy Carey, 4; Wayne Lynch, 7, 19, 36, 40. /*Valan Photos:*Michel Bourque, 8, 27; Stephen J. Krasemann, 11, 16, 24, 28, 43; Dennis Schmidt, 23; Esther Schmidt, 32, 39, 46. /Bill Ivy, 12, 44. /*Visuals Unlimited:* Tom Walker, 15; Joe McDonald, 20; John Demske, 31; P. Lindholm, 35.